The

Power Of

Forgiveness

i

The

Power Of

Forgiveness

Dr. Dee Black

The Power Of Forgiveness

\

The
Power Of
Forgiveness

ALL RIGHTS RESERVE

Unless otherwise indicated all Scripture quotations are taken from the King James Version of the Holy Bible.

Editorial Note: Because we do not wish to give the enemy any additional attention, we have chosen not to capitalize any of his alternative names in this work.

ISBN: 13:978-1523287659
ISBN: 10:1523287659

Dedication

To My Lord and Savior Jesus Christ

This book is dedicated to everyone who is having a problem or who has had a problem with unforgiveness and is having difficulty embracing the truths surrounding Forgiveness. Prayerfully after reading this book, you will be in a better place with God, which will allow you to see what you are refusing to let go of is really holding you back from your God given destiny.

Acknowledgements

Sometimes the most necessitous and demanding task for a writer is transferring their thoughts from their heart to the paper. Thanks be to God that these struggles are softened and the tension is eased when they are surrounded by individuals that support the work that they are doing.

I am so grateful to God that He has surrounded me with people that love and support me while making my task easy.

I am thankful yet again for the opportunity to empty myself of a few nuggets that have helped me to overcome many obstacles that I thought were unreachable as well as unbearable, but God!

My deepest gratitude goes out to several influential preachers who afforded me the opportunity to sip from their proverbial saucers, and whose love for God's Word and stimulating conversations has kept my Spiritual candles lit and continuously burning. I want you to know you are a very important part of my life.

Bishop Carrie "CeCe" Cox, my sister and friend, my heartfelt thanks for all of your diligence in helping me to accomplish my vision and purpose for the Kingdom, I love you!

Prophetess Delaine Smith, my sister, and friend, for your unwavering love and support to me. For teaching other Ladies by example and Men from the Word of God to walk by Faith. I love you and thank God for you.

Thanks to the greatest people that God created, the **Sons and Daughters of Total Praise Christian Ministries.** Your love and support are above anything that I could ever imagine.

The Prayer Warriors and Intercessors: Thank you for keeping me lifted high on God's Help list. The Golden Girls: **Mother Patricia Walker, Mother Emmise Riley, Elder Dr. GeraldiNee Kirtsey, and Pastor Archie Colbert.**

Thank you for your unconditional love.

Pastor Calvin Williams and **Pastor LaTonya Walker** the **TPCM** Leadership Team: **Elder Barbara Hayes, Elder Raymond Riley, Minister Shirley Woodard, Minister Eric Brown, Lady Justine Brown, Minister Jessie Lumpkin, Minister Kizzie Griffin,** and **Minister Ebony Brown.** Thank you for all of the sacrificial work and support to not only the church but to Me.

Last, but certainly not least, my trusted assistants: Minister Kathy Lumpkin and Andrea Jones, thank you for your untiring support and making sure that I have what I need to make my assignments easy. Thank you for being the Diamond and Ruby with a willingness to serve.

Foreword

By

Bishop Michael D. Johnson

I take great pleasure in writing this review of what I would call a "Great work of transformation." When I read the text of this script, I began to understand how unique Dr. Delores Black really is. It takes a revelatory awakening to understand the power of forgiveness. It is one thing to intellectually extract principals of faith from the Holy Writ concerning forgiveness but to apply those principles to your life is the real testimony and power of oneself. Dr. Black's personal assessment of the hurt and pain of her past reveals to us that only the Word of God can free us from the condemning and destructive behavior of Unforgiveness.

Who are you helping most when you forgive the person who hurt you? I've come to understand that actually, you're helping yourself more than the other person. I always looked at forgiving individuals who hurt me as being really hard. I thought it seemed so unfair for them to receive forgiveness when I had gotten hurt. I got pain, and they got freedom without having to pay for the pain they caused. Now I realize that I'm helping myself when I choose to forgive. Dr. Black has chosen to forgive, and she has chosen to reveal to you and me how she did it. Many people ruin their health, and their lives are taking the position of bitterness, resentment, and unforgiveness. Matthew 18:23-35 tells us that if we do not forgive people, we get turned over to the torturers. If you have a problem in this area, I am sure this book "The Power of Forgiveness" will deliver to you the prescription for years of self-loathing and the harboring of hate.

Dr. Black not only gives us a Bible lesson on forgiveness, but she is a living walking testimony who practices what she preaches.

Congratulations on such a grand addition to the literary community. I'm so proud of you Daughter.

Bishop Michael D. Johnson
Chancellor of the Episcopal Academy
School of the Bishopric & Ministry
School of Overseers & Adjutants

Table Of Contents

Part 1: Forgiveness

Part 2: Unforgiveness

Part 3: The Power of Forgiveness

Forgiveness Is not an Option

Introduction

The purpose of this book is to uncover the tales and present to you the truths about forgiveness and the effects of unforgiveness according to the Word of God. I pray that after you have read this book, you will have a clearer understanding of the effects and consequences of both forgiveness and unforgiveness. God placed this project in my heart several years ago, while a student at Seminary, my final assignment was to write a thesis. I chose to write about "The Art of Forgiveness." The most amazing thing is that I went through all the formalities, passed the class and did absolutely nothing else with the paper. I thought about it and soon forgot about it. This project couldn't be birthed out then because I wasn't ready. It would have been premature and no doubt about it, it would have been written from a heart that needed to be healed.

I was still very much infected and affected by the spirit of unforgiveness. Not only that, I wasn't in the right place with God to do anything that would help or benefit anyone. Well, I sent my secretary to my office, and she brought me back the unmarked notebook. I opened it up, and there it was the paper that I had written years before but never did anything else with it. As I fanned through the papers so many thoughts came back to my mind such things as being surrounded by some type of jealousy even as a child. But when I cried out to the God of my Salvation (El Yeshuatenu), He freed my mind and heart from the hurt, Pain and every bit of resentment that I had allowed to infiltrate my heart. Strangely enough at the time I didn't realize that I was growing weeds in and around my heart that was choking out the choking out the genuine that was suppose to reside there.

But God, being the gracious Father that He is, redeemed the time and allowed me time to come to myself. I needed to change my thoughts, attitude, and allow God to change my heart. I did as King David in Psalms 51:10. I asked God to "create in me a clean heart and renew the right spirit within me." I didn't ask Him not to take His Holy Spirit from me; I asked Him to refill me with His Spirit, and I am so grateful that He did. It is so important that we understand that God isn't obligated to forgive us until we repent and forgive others. To simplify this, you have a choice. You can choose whether to forgive or not forgive the people that hurt you. Something else you need to be aware of, people that have a hard time forgiving others will also have a hard time forgiving themselves. If you remember nothing else please remember this. When you hold on to resentment and any other form of guile, you are not hurting the other person, you are only hurting yourself. The best thing that you can do for yourself is to be true to yourself. You need to REPENT to God and follow the instructions in 1 John 1:9, which tells us, "If we confess our sins, He is faithful and just to forgive us our sins, and to cleanse us from all unrighteousness." Here again is a choice, If you intend to complete the process you must forgive, release and pardon everyone including yourself of all that has been done. If the process is not complete, you will find yourself repeating the incident all over again. Still relinquishing strength, power and control of you to someone else. So do yourself a favor so you can continue to experience and enjoy the favor of God. Forgive immediately and LET IT GO! So you can move forward in the plan and purpose that God has for you.

Forgive

and

You will be

Forgiven

Part 1:
What Is Forgiveness?

Chapter One
What Is Forgiveness?

For whatever reason, Forgiveness can be very tough to handle depending upon the degree of the hurt or pain that someone feels they have been subjected to at the hand or mouth of someone else. I believe it is fair to say, no one knows how you feel or have been made to feel when your heart has been penetrated, and your thoughts have been overshadowed by everything but love. First of all, let's look at the definition of forgiveness so that you might gain a better understanding of what "forgiveness" really is. According to the Merriam-Webster dictionary to forgive is: 1) to **give up resentment of**, or claim to requital for 2): to **cease to feel resentment against** (an offender): PARDON, RELEASE.

Forgiveness is a decision to let go of resentment and thoughts of revenge. If you allow the act that hurt or offended you to remain a part of your life, there is no way you will be able to loosen the grip or be able to focus on the positive aspects of your life.

When you have a clear understanding of Forgiveness, it can surprisingly lead to you having empathy towards your offender. You may even find yourself understanding why your offender may have treated you the way that they did. As you allow God to cut away the stony parts of your heart, you will understand more clearly why "hurting people will hurt people.

Forgiveness doesn't mean that you need to deny your offender responsibility for hurting you, and it certainly doesn't minimize or justify the wrong that was done to you.

Finally, this is a reminder of what Jesus told his disciples when He taught them to pray, what we know as the Lord's Prayer in Matthew 6:12, "...and forgive us our debts as we forgive our debtors..." and verse 14 tells us, "...For if we forgive men their trespasses, your heavenly Father will also forgive you..." As you study the Word of God, you will see that different Bible translations interchange the word "debt" with trespasses and "forgiveness" with remission. Whether you use any or all of the translations, the meaning is basically the same. When you make the choice to be obedient and release every evil thing that is within your heart; you have repositioned yourself to receive all that you need for you to be able to move forward with the plans and purpose of God.

This is probably a good place for me to share a few things that helped me, and I believe it will help you:

1. I had to purpose in my heart to pardon and release my offender and myself.

2. I had to let go of the weeds of contention, anger, and resentment that was growing in my heart. I let It All Go!

3. When I let go of the bitterness, I could completely embrace the **BETTER** that God had purposed in every area of my life.

4. I had to make a conscious decision to Move On. I reminded myself that God called me, qualified me, and justified me. So the question to myself is Why am I allowing my offender to stop me?

I had to decree and declare that I was free. I pressed pass my past and regain my strength in the Lord. Most importantly, I stopped looking for the apology that I knew wasn't going to happen.

What I was truly seeking is a Spirit of peace and I wanted to be back in that special place with God.

Last but certainly not least, try to reconcile with your offenders. If it is not possible, I believe I can say I understand what you may be struggling with. But regardless of who did it, what happened, and how you were made to feel, you still need to be the bigger person in the situation.

Remember, once your Forgiveness process is complete the opportunity to reconcile will be much easier to accomplish.

Pray this Prayer

Father in the name of Jesus, I have chosen to forgive _____ for

_____. I no longer want to suffer the unnecessary pain and sorrow of unforgiveness. So in the name of Jesus, Father, I take authority over my thoughts and my entire self and I ask You to help me to take authority over the enemy. And in the name Jesus and the power of the Holy Spirit, I take back every part of me that I allowed satan to use to gain power over me. In the name of Jesus, I take back my mind, attitude, my love walk and especially my Praise. I desire to please you, Father, as I serve you with my whole heart and in all that I say and do.

In Jesus Name, Amen

Chapter 2
Forgiveness is a Choice

"Forbearing one another, and forgiving one another, if any man has a quarrel against any: even as Christ forgave you, so also do ye." **Colossians 3:13 KJV**

I often think about how God breathe these inspirations to men so that they may give it to us to live thereby. Looking at the scripture above starting with the word "Forbearing," as I thought about it and searched Webster's dictionary for the definition, I felt it was important that we understand what this word means. According to the dictionary, Forbearing is to hold back, to show restraint/refrain and desist from; resist. To cease, shun or avoid. To be patient and or tolerant in the face of provocation. To show self-control; to be slow to retaliate. God's word also has something to say about forbearing.

The book of Ephesians 4:2 says, *"With all lowliness*

and meekness, with longsuffering, forbearing one another in love." I believe forbearance is closely related to/with forgiving even though they have different meanings, they both require you to hold back your act of revenge and to let the matter go. Although, God said to let it go, it is still a choice that you must make. The decision to obey and prosper or disobey and suffer unnecessarily, the choice is yours.

There isn't a person alive who hasn't been treated poorly by someone at some point or time in their life. It doesn't matter if the offense was major or minor, you have a choice. You can hold on to the wrong that was done to you, or you can get up, dust yourselves off, forgive, pardon and release your offender and **keep it moving**. The Choice is Yours.

Forgiveness is not an option; it is a choice. You have to make the decision. Are you going to be miserable or will you have unspeakable Peace?

It is highly impossible for you to grow Spiritually if you are holding on to what someone did to you. But if you pardon and release your offenders, and yourself from what was committed against you, you will no longer be a victim of your past.

I know that it's not easy to forgive when you've been treated poorly and made to feel uncomfortable. Allow me to tell you that Forgiveness is the key to your freedom if you want to stop feeling bad about how you were treated and made to feel at the hand and mouth of someone that has a problem with you. Forgiveness is a very powerful tool that God has provided for us.

If you allow yourself to be motivated by the Word of God it will keep you in right standing with Him. That's why Jesus said, *"Therefore if thou bring thy gift to the altar, and there rememberest that thy brother hath ought against thee; leave there thy gift before the altar, and go thy way; first be reconcile to thy brother, and then come and offer thy gift."* **Matthew 5:23-24 KJV**

You do not have to suffer for the rest of your life for the mistakes or errors of your past. What happened in your past does not define who you are or what your future or destiny will be? God is in the business of reconciliation, restoration, and restitution. He will restore all that you have lost, if you will seek Him, and believe and obey His Word. Also, when you make a decision to forgive, it should be final. No ifs, ands, or buts about it. Your choice to forgive is not about how you feel anymore, because you have grown past that stage. It's all about being obedient to God.

If you are in between decisions as to whether or not you should forgive your offender, I challenge you to do what God said. Don't allow yourself to be tossed back and forth any longer. Make up your mind and allow your decision to move from your mind to your heart that you want to be healed, delivered and set free.

Don't forget forgiveness is not about how you feel, it is a choice. Forgiveness is an act of your own free will. When you make a choice to forgive, it means you have:

1. Given up the right to get revenge.

2. You've set aside all your resentment.

3. Stopped allowing what happen and the offenders to control you.

4. Stopped talking and rehearsing the offense.

You must also pray for your offender and hope that everything that is associated with them is going well. There is another thing about forgiveness being a choice I want to share with you. If you are still trying to wrap your head around whether or not your offender deserve to be forgiven, let me give you something to think about.

"For when we were yet without strength, in due time Christ died for the ungodly. For scarcely for a righteous man will one die, yet peradventure for a good man some would even dare to die. But God commendeth His love toward us, in that while we were yet sinners, Christ died for us." **Romans 5:6-11**

When you look back over your life, did you deserve to be forgiven by God and He allowed Jesus Christ to pay the penalty for our sins. If you are going to judge start with yourself.

Chapter Three
Forgiveness is a Process

Just so you know for the most part, forgiveness doesn't happen overnight. Forgiveness is a process. Before we move on, let's look at the definition of what a process is. According to Merriam Webster dictionary, *a process is a series of events that must take place in order for your conditions to change.* As you can see, a process isn't an overnight event and for your situation to change you must trust God for your transformation. Look at Romans 12:2, that tells us, *"...and be not conformed to this world; but be ye transformed by the renewing of your mind, that ye may prove what is that good, and acceptable and perfect will of God..."* Now you may be wondering why I took this turn, well because anytime your emotions are involved, you will need to trust God to help to clear your mind of the dark clouds and your heart of all the weeds. You don't want anything to hinder you receiving the complete forgiveness. What is complete Forgiveness? It is forgiveness that is free of ALL the weeds of contention, such as grudges, resentments, hatred, revenge, and yes, free of the residue. You may be wondering what is the residue? All of the thoughts and conversations that come to remind you of what happened. Understand this, a person may want to move past the incident; but because of emotional ties or restraints, they don't want to get caught in those snares again. You don't want to continue to let the negative agitations choke out your positive feeling, which ultimately takes you backward instead of forward. I can remember when I was younger and unsaved. I would go to the club with people that I called friends, and when we would have an argument, it wasn't for long because we knew how to get back together. You see when we forgave each other it made us feel right on the inside. There were also times when one of us wasn't entirely ready to forgive, but lied and went through the motions which caused us to have a dysfunctional relationship, which ultimately ended what we called our friendship altogether.

As you will see, throughout this book about how nearly everyone has been hurt by the actions or words of someone. Unfortunate as it maybe, if you don't develop a Spirit of forgiveness, you may end up being the one that pays dearly for an offense you didn't commit. Forgiveness is said to be good for the soul, and when you do it sincerely from your heart, you will find yourself in that special place with God, which is a great place to be. If you look back at the story of Joseph in Genesis 50, he had completely forgiven his brothers and found inner peace within himself. All though his brothers were afraid, when their father Jacob died that Joseph would seek revenge upon them for all they had done to him. What his brothers didn't know about him was that he was not only in a special place with God, he had a special relationship with God. I believed Joseph really loved his brother, and all though he was in a position that if he wanted to do harm to them, he could, Joseph's process was not only an evil experience, but God turned it around for his good.

"But as for you, ye thought evil against me, but God meant it unto good, to bring to pass, as it is this day, to save much people alive." **Genesis 50:20 KJV**

Remember this, as you go through the process of Forgiveness, don't forget your Purpose and why it is important for you to forgive.

Chapter Four
Jesus: Our Ultimate Example

There are many examples of forgiveness in the Bible, but this is one that I believe can serve as a reminder to us that no matter the situation or circumstances forgiveness is still the Godly thing to do. Our Lord Savior, Jesus the Christ, wasn't just an ordinary teacher or preacher; he was the greatest teacher-preacher. Jesus did what every Pastor/ teacher that counts themselves as great should do. They should allow his/her life to be an example of God's Living Word in action. Even though Jesus taught his disciples about forgiveness, He was also an example on the cross concerning what they had been taught.

The scripture in Luke 23:34, tells us what the first words that Jesus spoke as He was being crucified on the cross, *"...and Jesus said, Father forgive them, for they know not what they do."* Jesus was petitioning the Father to do the very thing that He had taught His disciples to do. In Matthew 5:44, the scripture tells us, *"But I say unto you, Love your enemies, bless them that curse you, do good to them that hate you, and pray for them which despitefully use you, and persecute you."* Jesus knew he would be treated unjustly and suffers on the cross, but even on the cross, Jesus represented the Kingdom of God very well.

Think about this, if Jesus could forgive the people that conspired against Him, mocked Him, beat Him all night long, and then nailed Him to the cross, why is it so hard for us to forgive and let go of the sufferings that we experience? Well I also want you to think about this, too. Do you ever think about the things that you have said and done to others, or do you think what you said or done weren't that bad and they just need to get over it. Well, allow me to remind you that what you did and the pain you caused is just as bad as the hurt and pain that you are enduring.

Forgiveness is not an option or about how you feel. Forgiveness is what we are commanded to do. Jesus said in Matthew 18:35, *"...if we cannot forgive others, we cannot be forgiven."*

I encourage you to be obedient and make the Godly decision to forgive others just as you have been forgiven.

Prayer

Father God in the name of Jesus, I love you and appreciate you for loving me and being my father. Father when I think about how You forgave the people that caused You to be the victim of their desires of that time. Then they had You nailed to a cross, and the only thing that You said was, "Father forgives them for they know not what they do." Father, you forgave them, so I am asking You to help me to sincerely forgive _____. Just as Jesus said, they didn't know what they were doing when they hurt Him. I want to have the same attitude concerning_____ they didn't know what they were doing when they hurt me. I don't want to hold anything in my heart against _____. I want to walk in love and fulfill the destiny that has been set for me.

In Jesus Name Amen

Chapter Five
Joseph: Our Godly Example

One of my favorite characters in the Bible is Joseph. He was the love child of Jacob and Rachel. Rachel was the woman he loved so much that he worked fourteen years so he could marry her. Joseph was born into a family of what we would call today "dysfunctional." Joseph was the little brother that God gave a dream that he couldn't keep to himself causing his older brothers to hate him. Joseph was the one that God guided through the process to prepare him to be second in command over a nation of his people. In Genesis 37 through the 50th chapter, there's an interesting story about Jacob and his son Joseph. He was the 11th son born to Jacob and the first son of the wife he loved, Rachel. God revealed His plan for the life of Joseph while he was still a young boy.

He told his brothers about his dreams; they were jealous of him and wanted nothing to do with him. He was thrown into a pit and left to die; then he was sold to the Gypsies. The brothers killed an animal and put the blood on the coat that their father had given Joseph, and then they lied to their father telling him that Joseph had been attacked and killed by a wild animal. They told him they were only able to salvage his coat that he had made for him, which they hated. Hate was all around Joseph. Several things happened to Joseph, he was eventually bought by a man who gave him great freedom even though he was a slave. He gave Joseph charge over everything he owned except his wife. While working, Joseph was falsely accused of a crime and ended up in prison. Joseph's integrity won him favor with the jail keepers, and he was given charge over the other prisoners. Over the course of time, God's favor allowed Joseph's dream to be fulfilled, and elevating him to a high position of power within the kingdom. The brothers thought Joseph was dead. They did not suspect that the man they would be bowing and standing before was their brother Joseph. When Joseph revealed himself, they were shocked to know he was alive. They even feared for years that he would seek retribution. After the family had been united, they lived together in Egypt. When their father passed away, his brothers began to fear even more that Joseph would finally show his hatred and revenge towards them (Genesis 50:15). Joseph was heartbroken when he learned his brothers still did not trust him, and they feared what he would do to them (Genesis 50:17).

It's amazing that people haven't forgotten how they treated you or wronged you, and how they think or feel that you still want to get them back

For what they have done to you. If you have forgiven your offender and moved on, don't allow them to take you back to that dreadful day or time because you may not be able to recover. If that happens, the enemy would have won. When you forgive and move on you are the winner because you have been empowered to authorize someone else to do what you have done.

This great story of forgiveness culminates with the words from Joseph to his brothers.

"Now therefore, fear ye not; I will nourish you, and your little ones. And he comforted them, and spake kindly to them." **Genesis 50:21 KJV**

We as Christians must allow our humility to be seen and our love for God which we possess to be felt. No matter the situation or circumstances surrounding what happened in the past, you shouldn't allow it to continue to infect or affect your relationship in the future. If your enemy needs bread, feed them. If they need shelter or clothing, help to make provisions for them. You should always be the bigger person in your way of thinking and living. I thought of our First Lady of the United States Michelle Obama in her powerful speech during her campaign journey for the Presidential candidate Hilary Clinton, she said, "When they go low, we go high." When I think about how Joseph's brother treated him, even throwing him into a pit. But when they experienced a famine in the land and traveled to Egypt for food to eat, Joseph put all of his feelings aside. He made sure that his brothers and his father that they left behind in Canaan was brought to Egypt for food and shelter.

I don't have to remind you of what you experienced especially from people that say they love and care about you. Perhaps you've had to deal with spirits such as jealousy, envy, resentment, malice, slander or maybe some other spirits that are not mentioned. But despite it all, none of these spirits are greater than the Power of God's Spirit.

Prayer Quote

"For they shall all know me from the least

to the greatest, declares the Lord.

For I will forgive their iniquity,

and I will remember their sins

no more." Jeremiah 31:34

Part Two:
What Is Unforgiveness?

Chapter Six
What is Unforgiveness?

The definition of unforgiveness according to Webster's dictionary is when an individual is unwilling or unable to forgive. I would like to look at unforgiveness as cancer. We all know that cancer can and will eat you up from the inside. I want you to allow me to share with you the stage that I came to know. The first stage can be very invisible to the point that you have no idea that it is there. You know you feeling some kind of way, but this is the stage that is mostly overlooked. For the spirit of unforgiveness, I like to call this stage denial. What is denial? Denial is when you don't accept or pretend you don't know what's going on within you. As unfortunate as it is, most of us at some time or the other have experienced this stage. But when discovered, it can be devastating. If the spirit of unforgiveness is not dealt with in a timely manner it can turn you into a very hateful individual. The attributes of unforgiveness is not new. Let's look at what happened in the Garden of Eden. In Genesis 4:3-8, is where the first murder took place. But leading up to that incident, Cain had a grudge against his brother Abel. Even though it was God that accepted Abel's offering and rejected Cain. As sad as it is, unforgiveness still leads to unnecessary resentment, grudges, retaliation, and hatred against others. Yes, hatred. Hatred is like a sore that is infected and festering when the scab is knocked or picked off. The more you pick at the scab, the more infected the sore becomes. Think about this, the more you allow your mind to be consumed with what happened, the more you become consumed with getting even or revenge with the person that hurt or offended you. Individuals whose been hurt or offended and have unforgiveness in their hearts enjoy having a poor me party. The guest that attends makes them feel justified in wanting to take revenge on their offenders. They are very cunning as they tell others how cruel they have been treated. They intentionally do this so others will feel sorry for them and agree that what they have planned to do is justified. Do you know anybody like that? Look at this story. There was once a little girl in our church. She was smart, but she had a lying and deceitful spirit. This little girl had a way of getting people to feel sorry for her. She was disobedient, but did not want to be corrected. She would do something at home and when she was disciplined, she would sniff all the way to church. When she got to church and as soon as someone looked at her and asked what was wrong she would turn on the tears. Now for what it is worth, it was never her fault and she always did everything right. Well during the course of time, this little girl grew up, and now had children of her own. I have watched her on several occasions, she is very stern with her children. I can't believe that she disciplines her children for some of the same things she once did, but she did not want to be disciplined. Now she is dealing with something that happened in her childhood that she is having a problem releasing. I told her about my book and she was very excited. I was very frank with her, in terms of her releasing and letting go of things in her past that she can do absolutely nothing about. I did let her know the choice was hers. The sad conclusion of this story is that she carries the illusion that someone else is the cause of her misery instead of accepting responsibility for her unnecessary torment and warfare. Don't allow this story to have your name in it. You don't have to be a victim of your past, Make up your mind that you will release, forgive, and forget the past that you can do absolutely nothing about.

Chapter Seven
The Danger of Unforgiveness

The Bible makes it very clear that we as disciples of Christ are suppose to trust and obey His Word. In Mark 11:25, it tells us what we are expected to do when we stand to pray.

"And when ye stand to pray, forgive, if ye have ought against any; that your Father also which is in heaven may forgive your trespasses."

I believe for you to understand unforgiveness, you must first understand what forgiveness means. The New Strong's Complete Dictionary of Bible Words gives several variations of the word "forgiveness," starting with the root word "forgive." Which means, *to cover, to expiate, to free entirely, to pardon, release, dismiss, to let go, and to set at liberty.* As you can see, according to Webster's dictionary the word and the scripture that Jesus used we are compelled to let go of the offender and the offense or to make it simply, we must forgive the wrongdoers and the wrong that was done. The moment you decide to hold on to the wrong that was done to you, is also the moment you made a choice to walk in unforgiveness. One thing that amazes me, it's how people will tell you about their walk with God. How they don't do this or that and how they want to go to heaven. They even talk about how much they love the Lord, but they never speak of the love or forgiveness of people. Mark 11:26, tells us that, *"When ye do not forgive neither will your Father which is in heaven forgive your trespasses…"* Think about what happens when unforgiveness enters your heart. I believe I can say; it becomes somewhat like erosion, which gradually eats away at your inner being. Making it hard to love or trust someone and it slays your ability to develop a genuine loving relationship with God or man.

Another reason people hold unforgiveness in their hearts, they think they are hurting the one that hurt them, but they're only adding injury and applying unnecessary pressure to themselves. I also want to make you aware of this, whenever you refuse to let go of unforgiveness, you have just opened the door to satan, and he doesn't have a problem building a stronghold. When you have unresolved anger and situations, it is easy for your mind and heart to become captive to the enemy's will. It's important that you know how dangerous unforgiveness is to not only your offenders but to yourselves. It leads to unfounded sin and a life separated from God. One of our greatest blessings of all is that Jesus, the Son of God, was made flesh and dwelled among men so that he could break down the walls of sin that separated man from God.

It is truly a blessing that Forgiveness is the major focus of the Gospel's message that was left as a guide to be followed by all that would embrace it.

*"To whom ye forgive anything, I forgive you also; for if Ii forgave anything, to whom I forgave it, for your sakes forgave I it in the person of Christ. Lest satan should get an advantage of us; for we are not ignorant of his devices. "***2 Corinthians 2:10-11 KJV**

I encourage you to stay away from the danger zone of unforgiveness because there are consequences you may not want to encounter or experience due to you wanting to do it your way. God's word is not a Burger King menu. You cannot expect to have everything your way.

Chapter Eight
Consequences of Unforgiveness

Jesus taught the disciples about forgiveness and the consequences of unforgiveness, and as followers of Christ, we are to abide by the teachings of Jesus as well. Both the Old and the New Testaments had stories concerning forgiveness and unforgiveness. This chapter will focus on the consequences of unforgiveness. Jesus warns us of the consequences of refusing to forgive anyone. Let's look at several Consequences of Unforgiveness.

1. Inhibits God from forgiving us.

"For if ye forgive men their trespasses, your heavenly Father will also forgive you: But if ye forgive not men their trespasses, neither will your Father forgive your trespasses." **Matthew 6:14-15 KJV**

2. Inhibits coming into God's Presence.

"Therefore, if thou bring thy gift to the altar, and there rememberest that thy brother hath ought against thee; Leave there thy gift before the altar, and go thy way, first be reconciled to thy brother, and then come and offer thy gift." **Matthew 5:23-24 KJV**

3. Inhibits God from Answering Prayers

"Therefore, I say unto you, what things soever ye desire when you pray, believe that ye receive them, and ye shall have them. And when ye stand to pray, forgive, if ye have ought against any; that your Father also which is in heaven may forgive you your trespasses." **Mark 11:24-25 KJV**

4. Being delivered over to the Tormentor.

"Shouldest not thou also have had compassion on thy fellow-servant, even as I had pity on thee?   And his lord was wroth, and delivered him to the tormentors, till he should pay all that was due unto him." **Matthew 18:33-34 KJV**

5. Inhibits you from being Spiritually Fruitful

"If a man abides not in me, he is cast forth as a branch and is withered; and men gather them and cast them into the fire, and they are burned." **John 15:6 KJV**

6. Inhibits you from getting into Heaven

"Not every one that saith unto me, Lord, Lord. Shall enter into the kingdom of heaven, but he that doeth the will of my Father which is in heaven." **Matthew 7:21 KJV**

These are a few of the consequences that need to be taken seriously by individuals that expect the blessings of the Lord. Please take note that God has no mercy on those that refuse to forgive and continues to sin. Just briefly at **"Being delivered over to the Tormentors."** The parable that Jesus talks about in Matthew 18:34, tells us about how a man begged to be forgiven and his Master had pity upon him a n d forgave his debt. But the man came upon a man that owed him money; he grabbed him by the neck and demanded his money. He was seen by another man that knew he had been forgiven; he went and told the Master. The Master sent for him and turned him over to the tormentors. We will also look at the root of tormentor which is torment. When you refuse to forgive the Lord can turn you over to the tormentors to be tormented.

Examples of Torment

1. **The torment of Sickness**: when you make a decision to hold on to unforgiveness in your heart, you have forfeited your claim to God's healing power. Isaiah 53:5; Psalms 66:18. The tormentor can attack any parts of your body when you have been handed over to him or her. Attacks such as depression, oppression, and other mental illnesses will take over your very being if it's unnoticed. But on the other hand,if you

want complete healing of your Mind, Body, Soul, and Spirit, you need to be sure to search yourself and make sure you aren't holding any unforgiveness in your heart.

2. The torment of Marriage and Family breakdown: Anytime there is unforgiveness in a marriage due to unresolved issues (the sin of deceitfulness, infidelity, finances, and domestic relations) between a man and his wife or vice versa a woman and her husband, there will also be blockages of God's blessings. Malachi 2:10-16, talks about covenant marriage to your lifetime partner and it takes a very stern look at divorce as one committing treachery. As you may know, there is no perfect marriage, but as the couple works on it daily it will be strengthen. Couples (a Man and a Woman) that are in a covenant marriage relationship must try with all that is within them to have a holy Covenant Marriage that is pleasing to God. It is so important for your marriage relationship to be strong and your communication with each other should the same as with God. You both should be able to talk about everything, leaving out nothing, and leaving no place for the enemy to come in unaware. Something else that must be considered, if children are involved in the marriage, they must be protected. The tormentors don't care who they hurt. Unfortunately, the one that has been tormented has a tendency to become a tormentor.

3. The torment of the Children: Unforgiveness can be the cause of misplaced anger and rebellion in your children. Most of the time all they want to know is "why"? It's amazing how adult children hate their parents for situations that occurred during their childhood. Jeremiah 31:29 and Ezekiel 18:2, speaks about the parents eating sour grapes and setting the children teeth on edge. It is so unfortunate, this is what has happened to the children. They are left with an appalling taste in their mouths while trying to recover from the lifestyle of their parents. The scriptures were written in Matthew 15:4 and repeated in Mark 7:10, along with Ephesians 6:1-3 these are the first scriptures written for children with promise. Children have a problem forgiving the past and letting go of the hurt, pain, and hatred towards the persons that hurt them. It's sad but true; they will not enjoy the benefits of what the Word of God promises because of their refusal to forgive. Some children think if they stay away from the parents, the problem will go away, but it doesn't. Some of them are looking for a simple thing like, "I'm sorry" for what I put you through. Even though it doesn't change anything, it just might change somebody's heart.

Never the less the scriptures still stand true as written. *"For God commanded, saying, Honor thy father and mother, and he that corset father or mother, let him die the death."* **Matthew 15:4; Mark 7:10 KJV**

"Children, obey your parents in the Lord, for this is right. Honor thy father and mother, (which is the first commandment with promise ;) That it may be well with thee, and thou gayest live long on the earth." **Ephesians 6:1-3 KJV.**

No matter what, children young or old must forgive, honor and respect their parents, if they want to be blessed by God. There is so much more that can be said about being handed over to the tormentors (satan and his demons). I encourage you to make a conscious decision to turn back to God with your whole heart as you repent, release, pardon, forgive others and above all forgive yourself.

Chapter Nine
Recognizing Unforgiveness in your Life

"For if you forgive men their trespasses, your heavenly Father will also forgive you. But if you did not forgive men their trespasses, neither will the Father forgive your trespasses." **Matthew 6:14-15 KJV**

Have you ever thought about this, if we are not forgiven of our sins, we have no hope, and certainly, there is no way for you to enter the kingdom of heaven? That is why it is so important that you understand the totality of what it means to forgive and be forgiven. My goal is to help people to understand the importance of forgiveness as well as how to recognize the signs of unforgiveness, which maybe in your hearts. Hopefully, by the end of reading this book, you will have a complete understanding about how to forgive someone from your heart. As you look at the scripture above, there is a promise in the message that Jesus makes very clear. *"For if you forgive men their trespasses, your heavenly Father will also forgive you: But if ye forgive not men their trespasses, neither will your Father forgive your trespasses."* **Matthew 6:14-15 KJV**

I believe unforgiveness in a person's heart is one of the main reasons why they don't make it into heaven. Allow me to tell you a story about a man name Andrew; he was a member of our church. He served and retired from the United States Armed Services. He was stricken with a stroke that left him partially challenged on his left side. Andrew was a strong-willed man that was determined not to let his physical condition stop him from doing what he wanted to do. He told me about how he stayed in the VA hospital for 30 days. On the day that he was supposed to be released, he had to be pushed in a wheelchair to the car. When he reached the front door, he told the nurse to stop and she did, and he stood up and walked out of the hospital to his awaiting car. He said if he had crossed the threshold in that wheelchair, he would have never walked again. As he continued to talk, I thought, what a determination. He was left with paralysis in his left leg due to the stroke; it slowed him down, but it didn't stop him. Andrew was a well dressed educated man that didn't mind helping or lending a hand to anybody in need. He set several goals and accomplished them all. The day after Thanksgiving 2012, we received a call that we needed to get to the hospital as soon as possible. I immediately started to pray in the Spirit, when we arrived in the Emergency Room, all of his immediate family was there. I spoke to them briefly before going to the bedside of Andrew. The nurse and the doctor that was on duty ask me if I was there to give him his last rites. I said, No! I'm here to speak life into him. I turned to Andrew and started to pray in the Spirit and his heart began to beat again. We all gathered in the chapel and prayed; then we went to the waiting room to wait. About two hours or so later, the Cardiologist came in to talk to us, he told us how he was contacted twice before making a decision to come to the hospital. He continued to speak to us about the surgery he had performed and said if Andrew made it through the night; he would have a chance of recovering. Praise God, Andrew made it through the night and was awake the next day when we arrived. I said all of that to get to this point. I couldn't wait to get to him so that I could talk to him about whether or not his heart was clean. I asked him if he had anything in his heart against anybody. He told me, in the name of Jesus, He didn't have anything in or on his heart against anybody. I thanked and praised God for allowing me the opportunity to make sure that Andrew had no unforgiveness in his heart. There was an incident that happened, the truth of the matter was never resolved. The night he was taken to the hospital, I got in his ear once again, I asked him if he had any unforgiveness against anyone, he motioned with his head, No! With tears in my eyes, I thanked God. Andrew gave up his fight to live that night, and a week later, God called him home. I am so grateful that there were no signs of unforgiveness in the heart and the life of Andrew. Now that we've read the story, we can see how important forgiveness is to our eternal salvation. Let's examine our hearts to make sure we have truly forgiven everyone from our heart. When was the last time you asked God to search you to see if you have any wickedness in your heart?

"Search me, O God, and know my heart; try me, and know my thoughts, and see if there be any wicked way in me, and lead me in the way everlasting." **Psalm 139:23-24 KJV**

I encourage you to do it, and when you do, if you see anything ungodly, please don't ignore it. **Clean it up**. Don't allow yourself to die a slow death from the poison of unforgiveness that have marinated in your heart, use your antidote. The antidote for unforgiveness is Forgiveness.

Pray this Prayer

Father in the name of Jesus help me to recognize and not overlook the anger, bitter, grudges, resentment, and the jealousy that is in my heart. I repent for overlooking my faults. And not walking in forgiveness with _____Thank you Father, for hearing and answering me. In Jesus name.

Chapter Ten
Unforgiveness will poison you Spiritually

Unforgiveness is like a poison that begins on the inside, and like an infectious disease, it can spread and infect the entire body. But all is not lost, and healing is available for you. Unfortunately, because of all the false myths about how hard it is to forgive someone for what they did or the hurt they caused, people end up holding on to the pain. Sadly to say, holding on to unforgiveness has caused more damage to them than the situation. Is there a cure for unforgiveness? Yes, it is. The cure is your choice to Forgive. I read a brainy quote some time ago which said, "Unforgiveness is like drinking poison and wishing someone else dies." When I read it, I thought it was the dumbest thing that could be written. I couldn't help, but to think about, the offender isn't dying, you are. Then I though, most of the time people hold on to situations as a security blanket, and on the other hand, they hang on to it because they don't know how to release it and let it go. Are you one of those people that think this way? If not, bless you. If you are, have you also convinced yourself that you have a right to do and feel the way that you are feeling? It's important that you know there is a cure. Unforgiveness is the most damaging poison that the enemy uses against God's people. It can cause serious damage to your spiritual walk if not taken care of immediately. Let's look at some of the ways can poison you spiritually.

Unforgiveness shows your lack of love for God and Man.

Jesus gave several commandments concerning our love walk. First our love for Him, in John 14:15, He says, *"If ye love me, keep my commandments…"* Then in John 15:12, He tells us of the love we should have for one another. "

This is my commandment, which ye love one another, as I have loved you." I believe I can simplify this by saying, if you don't keep Jesus commandments, then it becomes evidence, you don't love Him. Likewise, if you hold anger, bitterness, or unforgiveness against anyone, then you don't love as Christ loved you. Jesus goes on to say in John 14:24, *"He that loveth me not keepeth not my sayings, and the word which ye hear is not mine, but the Father's which sent me."*

Unforgiveness forfeits your forgiveness

As Jesus were teaching His disciples to pray, in Matthew 6:12, He tells them to forgive to be forgiven. *"...And forgive us our debts, as we forgive our debtors."* and in verse 15, He speaks about what will happen if you refuse to forgive. *"...But if we forgive not their trespasses, neither will your Father forgive your trespasses."* Simply put, if you want to be forgiven, you must forgive.

Unforgiveness can defile you

The scripture in Hebrews 12:15 tell us, *"...lest any root of bitterness springing up trouble you, and thereby, many be defiled."* It is very clear that many will be defiled if the bitterness of unforgiveness takes root in their heart.

Unforgiveness gives satan an advantage

When you refuse to forgive, it gives satan an advantage over you that he shouldn't have. 2 Corinthians say it like this, *"To whom ye forgive anything; I also forgive; for if I forgave anything, to whom I forgave it, for your sakes forgave I it in the person of Christ…"*

Unforgiveness can keep you out of Heaven

According to Matthew 7:21, *"Not everyone that saith unto me, Lord. Lord, shall enter into the kingdom of heaven, but he that doeth the will of my Father which is in heaven."* Just because you call on the name of the Lord, you're getting into heaven? You must REPENT, TURN YOUR HEART BACK TO GOD and DO HIS WILL.

Unforgiveness prevents your Spiritual Fruitfulness

The way for you to be fruitful is to abide in Christ and keep His commandments. John 15:5, *"I am the vine, ye are the branches; He that abideth in me, and I in him, the same bringeth forth much fruit…"*

There is an antidote for the poison of

unforgiveness. Your forgiveness towards others opens God's forgiveness towards you. When you REPENT and walk in FORGIVENESS, you become living proof of God's miracles and blessings.

Part Three
The Power of Forgiveness

Chapter 11
Forgiving yourself and Others

This has been one of the most difficult tasks that I have ever encountered. Writing these chapters has allowed me to reflect on the past and evaluate how and what I could have done differently. It's been a challenge. Not because I haven't forgiven the people or myself, but because I want the precepts of this process to be understood. As a pastor, I have the privilege of meeting some phenomenal people. A few weeks ago, I had the opportunity to talk with one of my spiritual daughters. This girl is gorgeous but very insecure. She started out very young looking for love in all the wrong places. We talked about things such as why she attracts men that mean her no good, why she can't seem to have a permanent relationship that will lead to a covenant marriage, and then we talked about things in her childhood.

Only to find out this is where her problems started and she is having problems dealing with them now. While talking about whether she had forgiven the people that hurt and disappointed her, I guess I hit a nerve, she started to cry and say, 'she could never forgive him for what he did to her' and the more she talked, the more enraged she became. She slipped out of the chair down to the floor. She was screaming and yelling at the top of her voice; then she started to fight and suddenly, she stopped fighting and started asking the Lord to help her. I held on to her as she tried to stop crying. When she composed herself, she was like a new person. Then she told me about all the abuse that she experienced. She picked up her phone, dialed a number and started asking f o r forgiveness for everything she had done to them. She openly confessed to saying and doing evil things to the person; she asked them to forgive her for that, too. She said a few other things, and then she hung up her phone. She looked at me and said, "I was talking to my children's father." He is the one that I loved the most, and he is also the one that abused me physically, verbally, and emotionally, but now she was free. She told me that it had been a long time since she felt the way she did. We prayed that not only is she free of the unforgiveness but there will be no residue attached to her to remind her of what happened to her. We prayed that her relationship with God would be renewed. She said she couldn't imagine ever being free because she had been bound for so long. Well, that day was a day of freedom and forgiveness for both the parties involved. They have since moved on, and seem to be enjoying married life. To forgive yourself and others. You must make a conscious decision to forgive the other person and yourself, release the other person and yourself and let it go and BE FREE!

Exercising these steps will help you to forgive yourself and others quickly.

Face the situation and Free yourself.

Obey the Word of God to forgive.

Release the offender and the offense.

Go forward and don't look back.

Include your offenders in your prayers.

Vindicate your offender and yourself.

Exonerate yourself and the offender.

No longer will I hold on to the past.

Emanate a true Freedom of Forgiveness.

Spring forth from the darkness of sin.

Survive and thrive because you have chosen to walk in **Forgiveness.**

If you use these steps in your prayers and declare them over your life, you will experience a significant change like never before.

You may not be aware of this, but you have been given the keys and power to set yourself and others free from anger, bitterness, resentment, and unforgiveness. Now that you know you have the keys and the power to be set free, you need to do it. Your Forgiveness is not just for the one you need to forgive, it for YOU as well. **Try It!**

Prayer

Father in the name of Jesus, I desire to have a spirit of forgiveness. I desire to walk in love, obedience, and repentance towards God and man. I forgive_____ and the offense _____ and I vow to be rid of all the attributes of unforgiveness and embrace the forgiveness that is in my heart.

Father, I thank you for washing and cleansing me of all the unrighteousness that held me back from embracing the treasures that have been laid up for me. Thank you for forgiving me, In Jesus name. Amen.

Chapter Twelve
Write it Down and Off

Did you know that Church folk can push you to a point what seems like there is no return? But you've got to be in control of yourself at all times. Look at this story and see if you can relate. While fixing dinner for my family, I was watching TV, and a televangelist by the name of Marilyn Hickey came on. She was talking about how she had been personally attacked by a pastor, and she was furious about what he had said and done to her. In the meantime, she was invited to speak at a local church and when she graced the pulpit the preacher that has attempted to humiliate her was seated there, and the only available seat was next to him. She went on to talk about how uncomfortable she was. When she got home, she went to God about the problem, the

Spirit of God told her to write down everything she wanted to say to the preacher about how he made her feel. But this is the hit kicker; the spirit told her to write a letter to him. Write down everything she wanted to say and if she still had those bad feelings towards her offender to mail the letter to him, but if she reconsidered she needed to tear the letter up. Because of the God in her, she reconsidered and torn the letter up. But God always has a plan, and as He would have it, the preacher ended up contacting her to apologize. The more I thought about the situation, the more I knew I needed to suggest this process to the young girl in my church. There were two girls Dedra and Mary, they had an argument and vowed to have nothing to do with each other ever again. I had watched their relationship for a while. They were the same age, but Mary somewhat

controlled Dedra. That particular day, I guess
Dedra had enough of Mary, but she never
took the time to tell her how she had made
her feel. When Dedra decided to talk to me
about the situation, I suggested that she write
Mary a letter telling her all about how she
made me feel, and how she wanted to do
harm to her. Dedra said during the process of
writing the letter something happened to her;
the light came on, and she realized her
salvation was worth more than the weeds that
she had allowed to take root and grow in her
heart. She said she ripped the letter up and no
sooner than she did her phone rang and it
was Mary talking as if nothing had happened
between them. Dedra told me, she felt sorry
for Mary. Mary wanted to talk about old
times, but Dedra had been hurt by Mary and
she wasn't going into that situation again. I
said, so reconciliation is out of the question,

Dedra said yes. Then I said this is what I want you to do, she said, do what? I said, forgive them, and release them as well as yourself. She was silent, and then she said, why? That's when I told h e r if she wanted her ministry or whatever she decides to do next to thrive and be successful, she would have to forgive them, as well as herself for the part she played in a mess. I guess she decided to forgive them and herself because she seems to be doing well in her ministry. From that day I started using the writing method as a form of therapy for getting past hurts and disappointments. You will be surprised at what will come out of you, including what you did as you decide to become totally free. Don't forget forgiveness is a choice. Free your heart and mind and your body will surely follow behind.

Letter Writing Therapy

I want you to try this exercise. If you decide to write the letter using your electronic device or use paper and pen, the choice is yours. Just do it.

1. You will need to be in a quiet place so you can think clearly.
2. Pray and ask God to help you to use the right wording.
3. Write down everything that you have been feeling concerning what was said or done to you.

Remember, this is a letter and if you decide to mail it or if you decide to rip it up or burn it, make sure no one can read what you have written. This exercise is designed to clean your heart and clear your mind so you can be free.

Prayer

Father in the name of Jesus, thank you for the wisdom to understand that I need to move forward in my life. I understand I need to release myself from the past so I can move forward to the future. I release and let _____ go. I no longer want to hold on to what happen to me or how what happened made me feel. I repent for holding on to what happen to me and not allowing myself to trust anyone. Father, I was fearful and didn't want the same thing to happen to me again. I am grateful Father, that I have learned how to handle situations differently, no longer with resentment or anger, but with love and kindness. Thank you, Father that it is so and it is done. In Jesus name.

Chapter 13
The Benefits of Forgiveness

No matter how difficult it may seem to forgive someone who has hurt or wronged you, you still must be the bigger person that offers the forgiveness. Before I move on, I want to define what a benefit is. A benefit is a profit, to gain an advantage. So not only is forgiveness a command, but it is profitable to you, and you gain an advantage over the enemy. But why forgiveness is said to be so difficult. To make it simple, the injured person feels they haven't done anything wrong, and they should be the one receiving the forgiveness instead of giving it. Another reason is that it is hard to forget or let what happened to you go. I want you to realize that you are the winner of the benefits in any challenge when you step up and forgive the offender and the offense. Just as we benefit from obeying the Word of God, we also benefit when we don't allow the offense to control us, but we control how we will handle it.

Listed are a few of the benefits of forgiving.

1. Greater Spiritual well-being

Your salvation is one of the most important benefits that your willingness to forgive can afford you. If you intend to maintain your Spiritual Growth, it's important to learn how to forgive. To truly understand the benefit of a greater Spiritual well-being, a person must realize that he/she was lost and needed a Savior to redeem their soul from the wrath of God. It would be a shame to lose your Spiritual benefit because of unforgiveness.

2. Emotionally Stable

When you make up your mind to forgive someone for hurting and damaging you emotionally, you are positioning yourself for benefits that you never expected to come your way. While people are looking, and expecting you to go off the deep end, you are experiencing God in a special way like never. You are not dwelling on the past but living in your future. Your determination to forgive plus your commitment to God will drive you to work through the wrong that happened to get to the right that's waiting for you.

3. Happier Relationship

When I hear stories of people from the Christian community that are separating and divorcing, I can't help but feel confused about why they could communicate and work towards forgiveness. Then I thought their trust factors have been damaged. Therefore, couples are more apt to make their partner suffer for their wrongdoing, rather than vowing not to hurt each other anymore. If they could ever receive the right counseling from the right counselor, they may be able to rebuild their trust and intimacy with each other which will prove to be very beneficial to them both. Remember, forgiveness is something that you do for yourself to sever all emotional ties to what happened. When you chose to move forward, it is for your safety and freedom. There is nothing wrong with removing yourself from a situation that you are finished with, but there is something wrong when you stay in a situation and continue to suffer in silence because you don't know how to remove yourself. Forgiven is not an option, it is a requirement if you desire God's forgiveness.

Chapter Fourteen
The Power of Forgiveness

God's forgiveness is a pattern for forgiving others and ourselves. Our forgiveness of others is the measure of forgiveness we will receive from the Lord. Let me remind you of what forgive is and is not. Forgiveness is "to send forth, send away, a dismissal, release, remit, and pardon." Forgiveness is not "ignoring the sin, putting the offender on probation, or merely refusing to retaliate." To make it plain, forgiveness is not acting as if the offense didn't happen, but you have chosen to forgive and forget quickly and not allow it to affect or paralyze you. When God forgives us, he "blots out, forgets it, doesn't hold the sin against us, and the most amazing experience is that He receives the sinner that repents of their sin and turns back to Him. Likewise, we are supposed to forgive each other always. There is great power in forgiveness, but we first must have the power to forgive those that offended us. Because we have received love and compassion; we should have love and compassion towards others. As we look again at the most powerful words ever spoken by Jesus, which should have changed the destiny of mankind. But some who have been forgiven treat forgiveness as if it is something God is obligated to do. God is not obligated to do anything especially for those that refuse to do what He says. As you may be aware, there are people that have a hard time forgiving others. Sadly to say, these people also have a hard time forgiving themselves. The three words that reveal the depths of your love and relationship with God is love, accept, and forgive. The way you love, accept, and forgive people should be the way you love God. Take back your power. It's Yours.

The Power of Forgiveness

1. What is our pattern for forgiving others and ourselves?

    _____

    _____

2. What are the three things that God does when He forgives us?

    _____

    _____

3. What's in Forgiveness?

    _____

4. What should we have for others?

    _____

5. Why should we forgive? (Matthew 6:14)

    _____

    _____

The answer to this question is also your memory verse.

Memory Verse:

_____

_____

Your Personal Prayer about

Forgiveness

_____

_____

_____

_____

_____

_____

_____

_____

_____

_____

_____

In Jesus Name, Amen

Chapter 15
Bible Verses about Forgiveness

Ephesians 4:32 - And be ye kind one to another, tenderhearted, forgiving one another, even as God for Christ's sake hath forgiven you.

Mark 11:25 - And when ye stand praying, forgive, if ye have ought against any: that your Father also which is in heaven may forgive you your trespasses.

1 John 1:9 - If we confess our sins, he is faithful and just to forgive us [our] sins, and to cleanse us from all unrighteousness.

Matthew 6:15 - But if ye forgive not men their trespasses, neither will your Father forgive your trespasses.

Matthew 18:21-22 - Then came Peter to him, and said, Lord, how oft shall my brother sin against me, and I forgive him? till seven times? Jesus saith unto him, I say not unto thee, Until seven times; but, Until seventy times seven.

Matthew 6:14-15 - For if ye forgive men their trespasses, your heavenly Father will also forgive you:

James 5:16 - Confess [your] faults one to another, and pray one for another, that ye may be healed. The effectual fervent prayer of a righteous man availeth much.

Luke 6:27 - But I say unto you which hear, Love your enemies, do good to them which hate you,

Colossians 3:13 - Forbearing one another, and forgiving one another, if any man have a quarrel against any: even as Christ forgave you, so also [do] ye.

1 Corinthians 10:13 - There hath no temptation taken you but such as is common to man: but God [is] faithful, who will not suffer you to be tempted above that ye are able; but will with the temptation also make a way to escape, that ye may be able to bear [it].

Psalm 103:10-12 - He hath not dealt with us after our sins; nor rewarded us according to our iniquities. For as the heaven is high above the earth, so great is His mercy towards them that fear Him. As far as the east is from the west, so far hath He removed our transgressions from us.

Luke 6:37 - Judge not, and ye shall not be judged: condemn not, and ye shall not be condemned: forgive, and ye shall be forgiven:

Romans 3:23 - For all have sinned, and come short of the glory of God;

EPILOGUE

Forgiving someone is said to be one of the most difficult things that a person can do. Well, I believe it is safe to say, if you are refusing to do something you don't want to do, then yes, it is hard. The Bible provides you with answers and the inspiration to inspire you to do the right thing. It gives you the directions that will help you to obtain the peace and freedom that you need for your spiritual growth and this journey. I believe the most amazing experience you can have is when you learn that forgiveness isn't just to others, it is for you. Stop holding on to the past hurts, pains of disappointments and the people that you feel caused you to be in whatever situation that you're in. Release that weigh before it turns into sin.

LET IT ALL GO!

Allow your healing to begin now.

ENDNOTES

Chapter 1
Merriam Webster Dictionary
The Holy Bible
The Power Publishing Analytical Study Edition

Chapter 2
Merriam Webster Dictionary
The Holy Bible
The Power Publishing Analytical Edition

Chapter 3
Merriam Webster Dictionary
The Holy Bible
The Power Publishing Analytical Edition

Chapter 4
The Holy Bible
The Power Publishing Analytical Edition

Chapter 5
The Holy Bible
The Power Publishing Analytical Edition
First Lady Michelle Obama-Quote

Chapter 6
The Holy Bible
The Power Publishing Analytical Edition

Chapter 7
New Strong's Complete Dictionary of Bible Words
The Holy Bible
The Power Publishing Analytical Edition

Chapter 8
The Holy Bible
The Power Publishing Analytical Edition

Chapter 9
The Holy Bible
The Power Publishing Analytical Edition

Chapter 10
The Holy Bible
The Power Publishing Analytical Edition

Chapter 11
Brainy Quotes by Marianna Williamson
The Holy Bible
The Power Publishing Analytical Edition

Chapter 12
Televangelist Marilyn Hickey

Chapter 13
Merriam Webster Dictionary

Chapter 14
The Holy Bible
The Power Publishing Analytical Edition

Chapter 15
All Scripture are taken from the Holy Bible
The Power Publishing Analytical Study Edition

The Author

Dr. Delores Black also known as **Dr. Dee** is an anointed dynamic, multi-talented; Spirit-filled and led Woman of God. Dr. Black was ordained in 1999 as the Senior Pastor of Total Praise Christian Ministries, under the leadership of the overseer/founder Bishop Dr. David Black. She received a Bachelor's of Arts in Elementary Education in 1985. She continued her studies at Jacksonville Theological Seminary earning a Master's in Biblical Studies in 1994, and a Doctorate degree in Christian Psychology which was conferred in May of 1995. She ministers effectively in the office of the prophet, as well as the pastor/teacher. Dr. Dee was affirmed and commissioned as an Apostle on April 16, 2011. Apostle Dee is the wife of Bishop Dr. David Black

More Works by the Author

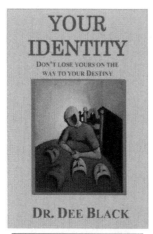

Contact Information

Total Praise Christian Ministries

2851 **Edgewood** Avenue North
Jacksonville, FL 32254
(904) 354-6900

Email address: drdee1216@hotmail.com

Cellular number: (904) 229-7170

The Power Of Forgiveness

Made in the USA
Columbia, SC
19 August 2018